Date Due

MY PARIS

MY PARIS

MY PARIS

MAURICE
CHEVALIER

PHOTOGRAPHS BY

ROBERT
DOISNEAU

FOREWORD BY M.F.K. FISHER

THE MACMILLAN COMPANY, NEW YORK, NEW YORK

COLLIER-MACMILLAN LTD., LONDON

COPYRIGHT © 1972 BY MAURICE CHEVALIER
PHOTOGRAPHS COPYRIGHT © 1972 BY ROBERT DOISNEAU
ALL RIGHTS RESERVED • NO PART OF THIS BOOK MAY BE REPRODUCED OR
TRANSMITTED IN ANY FORM OR BY ANY MEANS, ELECTRONIC OR MECHANICAL,
INCLUDING PHOTOCOPYING, RECORDING OR BY ANY INFORMATION STORAGE AND
RETRIEVAL SYSTEM, WITHOUT PERMISSION IN WRITING FROM THE PUBLISHER

THE MACMILLAN COMPANY
866 THIRD AVENUE, NEW YORK, N.Y. 10022
COLLIER-MACMILLAN CANADA LTD., TORONTO, ONTARIO

MAURICE'S SONG TO PARIS, "NOTRE PARIS," BY PERMISSION OF
EDITIONS WILLIAM MEYER, 9, PLACE MALESHERBES, PARIS 17, FRANCE

LIBRARY OF CONGRESS CATALOG CARD NUMBER: 75-163230
FIRST PRINTING

DESIGN AND PRODUCTION BY CHANTICLEER PRESS, INC., NEW YORK
PRINTED BY CONZETT & HUBER, ZURICH, SWITZERLAND
182/72/II/1

To the Paris streets of my childhood,
with tender thanks for having taught me life

Maurice Chevalier

CONTENTS

FOREWORD

DEAR MR. CHEVALIER:
BELOVED CHARMING DELIGHTFUL MAURICE:

Either way of addressing you is correct in my private Book of Behavior, for I respect you very much and I have also been in love with you since early in 1929, when I skipped college classes several times to educate myself, no matter how vicariously, in a movie house in Pasadena, California, where your first or at least my first American Chevalier was showing. (You sang "Louise.")

Then in the natural progression of an unrequited but still undying *affaire*, I found myself working one or two decades later in Hollywood, and I passed you in the hall of the Writers' Building at Paramount. That was too long ago for precise remembering, but it is certain that my scalp prickled and my heart quickened its beat before it seemed to pause a little. I would have liked to stop you in your starry tracks, but there was nothing to say to you except "Oh, Mr. Chevalier!"

The years went on, of course. One day when I was living in Aix-en-Provence I arranged to take my two young daughters and three even younger visiting nephews to Cassis. I had known it as an unfashionable tiny port long before the Second World War and had shunned revisiting it, not liking what I had been told about its changes: a casino, hordes of people, motels, snackbars.

But when we walked from our hotel to the Quai de Barthelémy, it was almost exactly as I remembered it: fishing boats dancing on the blue water and rubbing their sterns against the stone wharf, ready to sell their catch; flowers spilling from balconies over a café terrace.... It is still here, I said to myself. Nothing has really changed. War and even Time have not touched it.

There were the furled sails, the hawsers, the morning's shimmering catch ready to be sold, and the little terrace waiting for us to sit on it. Five lemonades and one pastis....

"Look," I said to my troupe. "This is where the rope is tied around the hawser to hold the boats safe to the quay." And I sat on one, and it was made of *papier-mâché* and plainly phony, and in a cloud of embarrassment, of mild mockery, I was led around the bend of the port to a big empty shaded terrace on the Quai des Baux, across the street from a café I remembered, or thought I did. There were sliced shadows across the tabletops, like the beach scenes from *La Dolce Vita*, and I felt lost in the flight of the years.

Somebody brought us drinks, after we had crossed the street to ask for them. We were told that *Fanny* was being shot, with Chevalier, Boyer, others. The plastic flowers, the old boats, the indestructible fish, the cardboard hawsers—they all fell into their own focus, and I felt less foolish, less fooled.

And then you, my dear Maurice, walked lightly under the thin bamboo roof and sat down at the other end of the empty open room from us, with two little girls. I knew you at once, and my heart jumped, then paused, and then lay still and waiting, exactly as it had in the dark Pasadena movie and the bright Hollywood corridor. You were as young, as superbly nonchalant and controlled, as subtly wise as ever.

Once more I pretended not to be there.

I have always been sorry for this final timidity. I am sure that there could have been a bright moment for the children and for me too, because you would have been courteous, as always, and we might have given you some fleeting amusement: five new people to smile blissfully at you, and at me their shy duenna. You would have recognized me, in spite of my obvious middle age, as another child crying out, "Look! There's Maurice!" You would once more have sniffed "the perfume of being human."

My two girls were sizing up the ones you were with, possibly a director's children, and there was that strangely wary atmosphere between our tables which, in older female lives, is kept less overt. One of my daughters finally murmured to me, "They are American!" She sounded a little top-lofty, and I asked mildly, "Like us?" She laughed and then said, "But the man is looking at you as if he knew you." I felt flustered, but answered, probably with an extra swig from my glass for courage, "He doesn't. But it is Maurice Chevalier!"

My girl gasped, in admiration and envy—of you, of me because you looked across at me so benignly, of life in general. All the children stared as politely as possible over the rims of their glasses.

Then is when I should have given you a genteel but still happy smile and walked across boldly to your table and said something silly, probably beginning with "Oh…." Yes, I should have done it. Our companions were all of an age, and it would have been good for mine to meet somebody from the country they had not seen for a long time. And I myself was old enough to do more than simply sit there in the stripes of sun and shade, my heart thumping, my hard-earned poise cowed by my admiration and my love for you!

I am reasonably sure that you were quite unaware of anything about that peaceful empty terrace except that you could relax in a quiet place away from the cameras for a while, with two nice kids and a few more across the shady way, sitting with their mother or nanny or somebody. If they stared a little, that was part of your way of life. But I, on the other hand, felt a wave, a current of real charisma-charm-empathy flow from you toward us, the kind that almost commanded me to walk toward you, smiling gently as you were smiling, warm as you were warm. Stupidly I let it turn into a Lost Moment.

This has always been a small sorrow for me, that I was so timid, so slow—afraid of spoiling your calm pause from the job, of embarrassing the children, of being politely removed by a bodyguard.

But now I have a chance to work for you, no matter how indirectly. Your publisher in America has suggested that, because of my real love for that young charmer well into his eighties when he wrote the book, I might like to write some sort of preface to your text. I could have shouted with joy. I need not wait for Heaven to be rewarded for my four full decades of devotion!

This is all right, culturally if not as a matter of strict decorum: I speak for countless women in my country—and for men too, who ask me with spontaneous candor to give you their love with my own. That is part of your ageless magic, that everyone who has ever met you, in a theater or movie or newspapers, seems to feel as pleasurably enamored of you as I do. You have written your own love song to Paris, and here is ours to you, in my words but for all of us.

Sincerely,

M. F. K. Fisher

Thine forever,

Mary Frances

LA CHANSON DE MAURICE

On nous transforme
Notre Paris
On le reforme
On le pétrit
L'ancienne image
De son visage
Tourne la page
Au fil des nuits
Depuis Lutèce
Il a séduit
Mais sa jeunesse
Est infinie
Pour ceux qui l'aiment
Il est le même
En d'autres termes
C'est notre Paris

A quoi bon regretter
Il nous a tant donné
Les hommes passent
Lui reste en place
Paris va Dieu sait où
Il survivra à tout
Car il sait rire
Aimer, souffrir

Pour Rome ou Londres
New York, Capri
Le bout du monde
Restera Paris

Quoi que l'on fasse
Il tient sa place
Rendons-lui grâce
C'est notre Paris

1. MY PARIS

Everyone has his own picture of this adored City of Light, whether he be a foreigner, a Frenchman, or a Parisian born and bred. For me, a child of the suburb of Ménilmontant, which, when I was born there in 1888, was a part of the belt of high hills around the great city, Paris meant only my own neighborhood of working men and artisans and their families. Many of us who were born there had never gone down into the heart of town, just as some country people never know any village but their own.

There were few hoodlums in those days before the turn of the century—very few crimes, thefts, muggings. We Chevaliers lived peacefully in our own little family circle. We had enough to eat. A small coal-burning stove warmed us in wintertime in the single room where my mother raised her three sons, my brothers Charles and Paul and me, the baby of the tribe. We knew what poverty was, but we were never in real misery. That was the way life had to be as far as we knew.

Sometimes we celebrated by going together on a Saturday or Sunday night to one of the popular *café-concerts* of our part of Paris: the Twentieth Century, the Belleville, the Labor Palace, or the Commercial. Their programs thrilled us, and the sight of the acrobats, the jugglers, the singers, plunged us into the marvelous world of their skills and their current song hits and dances.

A little later, when I was ten, we discovered the Cirque d'Hiver.

This "Winter Circus," still the most popular in all of Paris, seemed to us in 1898 a kind of family paradise. We could buy standing room for ten sous, half a franc, in a narrow gallery that lay behind the regular seats at the back of all the rising tiers, and there we would station ourselves, my mother and my brother Paul and I, clinging to the high railing as if we held hands with Happiness itself and were pledged never to let go. The show unfolded before us like a magic spell, an enchantment: the equestrian acts, the clowns and jugglers, all the acrobats, with Monsieur Loyal the master of ceremonies, the king magician of the rites.

One number, called "Francesco, death-defying bareback rider," left me paralyzed with admiration. Picture a handsome, dark young man in acrobat's tights, jumping onto the back of a horse at full gallop and then down again into the ring. He would leap once more onto the horse as it raced forward, but this time from a beautiful handspring, landing with his legs high and straight in the air. Once more on his feet on the horse's shining, surging back, with a *houpp* he would turn a complete somersault in the air and land with incredible precision as the two whirled at a gallop around the ring. I was literally obsessed by Francesco and his act—and no wonder, for he belonged to the Fratellini family, who became legendary in the world of the circus.

Two of his relatives, Louis and Paul Fratellini, were famous clowns and were among the biggest hits of the show. Louis, the talkative one, dressed in classical French ruff and spangles and wore a little pointed skull cap made of white felt. Paul played his stooge and, aside from his artistry as the traditional "fall guy," was an old pro at tumbling and jumping and knew every secret of a whirling somersault.

But it was the star tumbling act that thrilled me most. Here a boy exactly my own age stood on the feet of his father, who was lying on his back. From that position the boy was catapulted into the air and then caught in a perfect sitting position, hurled once more into a double somersault and caught again, finally sitting calmly back on his father's feet. The crowd would go crazy, and I screamed wildly as I saw myself in the role of the little professional, a traveling child acrobat.

After the performance we always went to the stage door on Rue de Crussol, where our favorites came out in their ordinary street clothes. We followed them on foot, thrilled to be that near to them, until they turned into a little tavern where they went to eat after their strenuous evening show. Then we would head happily back to Ménilmontant—walking, of course, to save bus fare. And then, in my dreams, I would be whirling and leaping and tumbling through the air in unbelievably dangerous patterns, clear to the limits of the Cirque d'Hiver's highest, farthest walls, while the spectators stood to a man and cheered me: "Bravo! Bravo, little fellow!"

In order to make this intoxicating vision come true, my brother Paul and I tried hard to exercise in all our free hours. He was a full-fledged metal engraver, while I was still an apprentice. Because he was older and taller, we decided that he should be the "heavy" and I the top man, the one who would do all the action. We had, of course, already settled on our name for the billboards: "The Chevalier Brothers."

Paul, who was thin and not very muscular, and I without the strength of a kitten in my little legs, progressed very slowly, even though we stayed fiercely loyal to our project. Fate did not see fit to let us go very far along the road to acrobatic fame. During one practice session I was supposed to rise to my full height as I stood on Paul's frail shoulders, do one somersault in the air, and land back, still standing, on his skinny forearms. Instead, my feet missed them and slid on down his back. My face hit at full speed against the back of Paul's head. He had to lead me home in a really pitiful state, with blood pouring from my nose and my face swelling and black and blue.

Our mother, La Louque, was horrified. She made us promise, with frantic pleas, not to go on with our efforts to be professional acrobats. With a painfully heavy heart I tried to adapt myself to the prospect of never being anything more than a workman in my future life.

But the germ of "show business," like a seed, had sprouted forever inside me, and another idea began to haunt me: Since I could not become an acrobat, because of my promise to my mother, why couldn't I try to be a singer?

And that is how it happened that one fine day in 1899, when I was eleven, I managed to get a free audition in a *café-concert*'s amateur show on the Boulevard de Ménilmontant. My performance brought forth a great deal of hilarity from my working-class audience. It was not because I showed any sign of talent but because I sang my song several notes higher than the pianist cared to accompany me! People were laughing themselves sick, and I knew it. But inwardly, inside my poor little soul, I told myself that I had, after all, made a beginning on the stage, all alone, and was not to be discouraged. "I have made the plunge," I said firmly. "The next step to be taken in my progress is to be sure to sing in the same key the pianist has chosen."

And so I began my career as a singer in the wrong key! Actually, the reason I became a musical-hall performer is that I did not have enough skill to be an acrobat!

From the top of our hill in Ménilmontant we could look down on the heart of Paris, as if we had seats in the highest balcony of a theater, from which we watched the tiny actors on the stage far below us. The city's wonderful monuments lent us, even so far away, some of their grandeur and their importance. Of course the brand-new Eiffel Tower, built in the year of my birth, was the first thing we saw and the biggest. Then there were Sacré Cœur dominating the hill of Montmartre, and the Arc de Triomphe, Notre Dame and the Louvre, with the Seine flowing sinuously between its banks.

This distant world seemed to us, even though we did not dare dream of braving it, like the private paradise of the bourgeoisie, the rich, the aristocrats and all their grand doings. It was the Paris of History. We others were actually like the peasants of the capital, humble and self-effacing, and as if held apart, kept in our places on the fringe. It is not that we felt like outcasts. We were simply the "little people," ill-paid, and remote from any way of life but our own.

We lived from day to day, sometimes from birth until death, in the narrow streets of our own quarter, and very few of us dreamed of being worthy of joining, sometime, those godlike beings who dwelt in their own celestial palaces, settings from a dream, another world.

Did any of us ever think of actually visiting the Eiffel Tower, standing in line for our tickets, waiting our turns to start the long upward climb, trembling with fear? We could look down on Paris from the first platform, and then the second, and then finally from the very top! Did it seem possible to us that we could be driven there by a lady-coachman in a carriage?

Could I have dreamed in those days that on my eightieth birthday the grandson of Monsieur Eiffel would present me with a reproduction of the famous building, thus covering me with both pride and confusion?

Sacred Heart, our Sacré Cœur seen from our own heights of Ménilmontant: How could we have known it any closer, with its gardens filled with sparrows, scattered restlessly now and then by lovers of every age billing and cooing exactly like the birds?

The banks of the Seine we knew only from our far hill when I was little. They still have their dozing habitués, who never seem to be afraid of rolling down into the turgid water which lulls them as they sleep. There is a serenity I know now when I cross the Pont Neuf, in front of the statue I never knew as a child, the Vert-Galant, good King Henry IV—and a fine feeling to be able to walk past the Conciergerie, a prison left from the Middle Ages which still keeps both its beauty and its veil of terrible drama.

One day when we were visiting places where I had once worked and played in Paris, Doisneau and I met a young boy who seemed to be imbued with a kind of distinction, a natural and inherent beauty. He was like a young prince, rising from the pavement of the Faubourg du Temple. He was pulling his fish net through the water along the edge of the Canal Saint-Martin, which had once served as a swimming pool to those of us who lived nearby. I asked the little fisherman, "What are you catching, kid?" He told me the blackish things hopping in his net were crawfish, and when I asked him what he planned to do with them, so small and dismally unappetizing, he said politely but with some astonishment at my stupidity, "Why, boil them and eat them, of course!"

(As I look with unabashed sentimentality at the photographs Robert Doisneau has taken of my Paris, our Paris, I cannot help smiling like a little boy at the mischief in his picture of one of the gargoyles of Notre Dame, which he has aimed so that the ageless devil is sucking the Eiffel Tower to sharpen its point, like a stick of sugar candy!)

And all that was and still is Paris, my own City of Light, as it quickly came to be called in the early years of its growth. What fairy godmother was it who blessed me with the good fortune, even when I was a little boy, to head straight for the heart of this paradise which seemed so unapproachable?

All alone, song by song, street by street, suburb by suburb, and then great boulevard by boulevard, I went my destined way and took root, at first brashly and then with more confidence as I was accepted. Finally, month after month and from one show to the next, and always successfully, I found myself, when I was barely twenty, hired as star in the most famous music hall in all Europe, the Folies Bergères!

My throat still tightens when I think of this first triumph, which saw me turn from a little Nothing-at-all, an unknown invader from the slums, into a promising Somebody among all the artists who have always seemed to me to be infinitely superior to me, except perhaps in their courage.

Already I had earned the right to say "My Paris," and now in my eighty-third year as I write about all this—now that I have deliberately given up the stage in France and the whole world, so that I need not fear that age itself might compel me to do so—I still keep in my heart the good memory of having lived through every mood and period of this magic place: the Belle Epoque, the Mad Years, and then Paris wild with enthusiasm and Paris sick and humiliated, Paris more celebrated than ever—and Paris singing the "Marseillaise," the "Internationale," the two songs separate and then together, Paris above all singing of Paris, of herself.

Behold the Medici Fountain and its drama of
jealousy! An individual named Polyphemus, driven
mad by the impossible blending of bronze and
marble, is ready to crush beneath a rock the two
young lovers, Acis and Galatea.

— Doisneau

2. THE VILLAGES OF PARIS

I often make little pilgrimages these days through the streets of Ménilmontant where I played when I was a child.

In our family I was seldom told what to do and what not to do. My mother worked from dawn until dark and often all night, while my older brothers and I slept without a care in the world, like secure young animals. Mother was too busy to preach any sermons about the dangers of street life as she slaved at her job as a seamstress in our one-room flat. Did she really know them herself? Besides earning our living, she kept us all clean and fed and clothed and tidy as well, alone at the helm after our father left us when I was eight years old.

My older brother Charles dutifully assumed his place as head of the family when he was only fifteen, and handed over to La Louque, as we called our mother (the nickname is meaningless to any but us, and infinitely loving and tender), all of his salary as a common laborer, except a fraction to cover his own small expenses and his Sunday outings.

My brother Paul, five years older than I, was still only a half-worker, somewhere between an apprentice and a full-fledged artisan, pulling in only a third of the regular pay. Of course he too brought it all home on Saturday nights, except for a tiny portion which he kept as Charles did for his private needs. I, at eight or nine years, did nothing but take, accept.

Everything else depended upon the ceaseless work and sense of responsibility of La Louque. I already knew that she was the real saint among us. Already, inside me, were the roots of an admiration and love for her which grew steadily deeper as the years passed. Why do I tell of this now? It is to make clear my first steps in those streets of what really amounted to a little working men's village, Ménilmontant in the last decade of the nineteenth century.

My life as a human being and a Parisian began in Number 31 Rue du Retrait, where I was born to a Flemish mother and a northern French father. What is left of my birthplace, a crumbling hovel when photographed for these pages, must by now have been torn down, or soon will be, as is happening to so many poverty-ridden ruins of my old Ménilmontant.

Our second address was in the narrow street called Julien-Lacroix, where Number 15 now carries the pompous title of "Hôtel de la Poste," and upstairs one flight, on the right, is the single room where the whole Chevalier family managed somehow to live together after our father ran off.

It was about then that I was beginning to learn all the games little poor children played in the church square, the Place de l'Eglise. I have never tried to find out how such a handsome and commanding building came to be erected in such a modest part of Paris. It still is, in my own judgment, one of the most beautiful churches in the world.

We played every possible game of childhood in front of it: Hide and Seek, Run Sheep Run, Leap Frog. I was already practicing the tricks I had seen little acrobats do in the music halls, balancing and dancing on the benches in the square and then on a pile of sand at the corner of the Rue Sorbier. I was foolhardy enough to try cartwheels and the beginnings of real somersaults. I was far from gifted and my legs were spindly, but I managed somehow to appear superior to the other kids in my crowd. I was already fighting strong feelings of inferiority, and I almost knocked myself out trying to prove, physically and in my own mind, that I was the opposite.

My horizon grew wider. I gradually came to know the Rue Julien-Lacroix and its little shops, where I did errands for my mother, and the Rue des Maronites, where the baker always gave me a leftover *croissant* when I bought our daily three-penny loaf of fresh bread. On the Rue de Ménilmontant there was the horse-meat butchershop, and when I bought our meat there the boss would cut me a good slice of delicious sausage. At the creamery, though, which was right across from our house, nobody ever gave me anything when I went in on an errand. I was shocked by this lack of common courtesy, as it seemed to me, and I never understood it, unless it proves that some merchants are nice to little people and others are not!

That narrow street, where just lately I tried to recapture a part of my childhood as I leaned against a telephone pole, proves by the modern building being constructed at one end that a new architecture has moved in and that it begins to reject any memories of the past. They must continue to live in my heart.

A little after the Rue Sorbier, which I knew from the top of the Rue de Ménilmontant, was the Rue Boyer where I was accepted by a private school directed by Catholic priests and where I did my first lessons and, always as a day student, stayed for several years.

Ménilmontant seemed to grow larger in my childish sight, with its main street and all the shops filled with shelves of their goods. To me it was like our great Avenue de l'Opéra. And the Rue Sorbier, which led to the Place Gambetta, where our town hall stood, imposingly laid out, seemed almost to try to push aside our beautiful church. How handsome I found it all!

La Louque often treated us, on Sundays, to a little party on the shady terrace of a big café called Les Tamaris, near the Place Gambetta, where we drank a small beer all around and nibbled at a big serving of crisp fried potatoes. We walked there and back home again, always stopping on the way to admire one part or another of the legendary cemetery of Père-Lachaise.

Once I had climbed up the Rue de Ménilmontant, to where it met the Rue des Pyrénées, my world grew ever wider. From there I could go to the Place de la Nation, and then on to the Bois de Vincennes, a poor man's Bois de Boulogne even in those days, when it was still admirably enhanced by the flower shows, which turned the woods into dreamlike bowers of exquisite blossoms of poetry.

At the other end of the Rue de Ménilmontant, much like a blood brother without any resemblance to his sibling, the Rue de Belleville existed in a more sophisticated and Parisian way than ours. On Belleville, things went on at a much faster speed, with a majority of good serious working people but also with a growing feeling of activity in all the shady kinds of perversity, which little by little I had to be aware of.

Have you observed how all that which is, no matter how subtly, a little more heavily spiced than humdrum life is more seductive and attractive? It may give you an idea of my increasing curiosity about life, although I was hardly out of my "baby" years and quite innocent mentally, if I describe to you the widening sphere of my wanderings.

Rue de Belleville led clear up to the fortifications of Lake Saint-Fargeau, where curiosity soon led me, and then, as I went down through the Faubourg du Temple, were spread out before me the Place de la République and its beautiful monument to Labor, a gigantic and proud goddess still reminding one of another Statue of Liberty, but lighting Paris and its suburbs instead of the harbor of New York.

The Place de la République is a major intersection where the great boulevards take off for the heart of Paris and the Opéra, and of course the Rue du Temple, which ends at the Seine, and the Avenue de la République, which rejoins on its right Père-Lachaise and on its left Ménilmontant. By the Boulevard Voltaire one could go to three of what were called "people's meeting places": La Nation, La Bastille, and the Bois de Vincennes. On the other side of Belleville the municipal slaughterhouses came first, a part of La Chapelle, where I sometimes ventured but always with a little feeling of panic.

In these rough, crowded, vital districts, peopled by hard-working and hard-living Parisians of every degree of human decency, I came to learn, just like a boxer, how to dodge, to guess, and to avoid as many knockouts as possible in the fight for life that shapes pure and inquisitive children just as surely as it does the reckless adults who have already been beaten in the haphazard pattern of man's destiny. It was natural that from my surroundings in Paris, when I was a little street kid, I formed a very good idea of everything I came to know later as a performing artist and even more as a citizen.

Of course, "my" part of the great metropolis has changed enormously in the past few years. Physically these areas have been partially rebuilt, giving to our former "inner towns" some of the feelings of certain parts of Brooklyn or Greenwich Village and mixing ethnic customs drawn there by the deathless grace and freedom of Paris herself. Some streets, though, almost like those of villages within the great city, still seem to hang on to their human characteristics and their truths, as if they were determined never to have anything to do with the Paris that changes every day and that never ceases to become something else, while staying the same place of beauty.

In Ménilmontant, as in most other suburbs, there is not the anonymity of a more fashionable neighborhood. People who live on the same street usually know one another. And so, if the house seems a little small, a person can always stretch out beyond his walls into the street itself. This is what the women do who gossip on doorsteps.

— Doisneau

63

Pages 47, 48, and 49
Ménilmontant.
Pages 50 and 51
The Auvergnats, merchants of wines and
charcoal.
Pages 52 and 53
Ménilmontant: 31 Rue du Retrait, the house
where Maurice Chevalier was born on
September 13, 1888.
Pages 54 and 55
In a bistro near the slaughterhouse of Villette.
Page 56
The Rue Julien-Lacroix in Ménilmontant.
Page 57
In two small rooms in this house on the Rue
Julien-Lacroix—now the Hôtel de la Poste—
Maurice Chevalier lived as a child with his
mother and brothers.
Page 58
Quai Jemmapes, over the locks of the Canal
Saint-Martin.
Page 59
Rue Laurence-Sevart in Ménilmontant.
Pages 60 and 61
Barges rising in the locks of the Canal
Saint-Martin.
Page 63
Canal Saint-Martin.
Page 64
A First Communion at Saint-Germain-de-
Charonne.

3. THE CHILDREN OF PARIS

Poor children on the hill at Belleville and in the streets of the working-class suburbs....

Artists' babies in Montmartre...

Comfortably middle-class children in the Parc Monceau...

Rich children in the Tuileries Gardens...

All these kids are drawn to one another, in their own surroundings, without any particular reason or explanation. They like to play together, or now and then seek each other out with a mysterious need that science has not yet identified. It is exactly in the way that innocent love affairs of little children resemble the instinctual actions of baby animals.

Poulbot's children, whom this fine painter and illustrator spent his long life depicting as true "street kids," were sketched from life, in full speed and fever, with all their mischievous nature and their unpredictable soul. Filthy, snotty, unkempt, irresistible and utterly moving in their spontaneity, they are adorable in their suggestions of the future and in their sensitive little faces.

The fathers and mothers of big families have enough to do, taking care of their own broods, and pay little attention to their neighbors' children, any more than they do to those they meet casually on the street. But grown-up people who have been robbed of parenthood look at these gamins, their eyes moist with a kind of painful frustration, turn back to look again with a strange poignancy at a handsome little boy or a pretty girl-child, and then follow their retreating steps.

Life has never given me a small angel of my own, and I feel over and over again, in the autumn of my life, this call, this astonishing attraction, this deep emotion on catching the look on a little child's face as I pass him, while he holds onto his mother's hand or his father's big fist.

It often happens that a five- or six-year-old who has seen me on television will grab at his father's sleeve or the soft grasp of his mother and cry out, "Look! There's Maurice!" And his parents will smile, and I will walk up to them and gently pat the little boy, who stares at me with his great, pure eyes. I'll congratulate his father and express my delight at their marvelous child, and then we will go our own ways, they pleased and amused and I with a little pinching of my heart, as if I needed more oxygen.

How many of these children stop me, or their parents! I admire them as they watch me with a gentle pleasure. I pay a compliment or two. It is one minute when I sniff the perfume of being human.

I have always been able to play uncle to my little nieces and the babies of my friends, but, in general, have never been able to keep up any real communication with them once they have passed their tenth year. They keep on loving me, I think, but their spirits leave me for their own dreams and those of their books, their new learning, what they glean from television and radio, what their peers add to all the budding thoughts in their heads.

At home now, in the house named for my mother, a boy of about nine called Laurent, the son of my gardener and his wife, who cooks for me, has become our favorite. He is very beautiful, endlessly inventive as he plays the little clown for us, constantly showing, in what amounts to gusts of affection, his strong sensitivity to us. I am literally in love with him. Will this last? I savor every moment of it and appreciate it, for he lights our existence at La Louque.

There are miracles and revelations, of course. For instance, there is Brigitte Vals, the daughter of François Vals, my business manager. I was almost unaware of her when she was very little, but suddenly she is around fifteen, wise, a hard worker, a thinker, wearing glasses and her own kind of beauty, and she appeals to me with an honesty of real rapport. So…you see that one can never tell!

Something that has always interested me about the children of working people in Paris is that no matter what district they come from, they are always playing war.

Playing? No! They are *making* war—and this goes on no matter what kind of quarter they live in. One street fights against another street. There is always a leader chosen naturally by the equally natural elimination of the bully of his area, and the weapons change in keeping with the times. In my own days we fought with our belts (not I—I was too scared), and then later came bicycle chains, and then rubber clubs, and then…

There was always some pretext for getting rid of our latent childish hatreds. It was almost as if the instincts of these sucklings still needed to satisfy themselves by biting, hitting, giving pain to the breast that fed them. Sometimes battle casualties were carried off the field in serious condition, but the victims were always proud of their wounds.

There are many young people of our capital who are more fortunate than the little urchins I lived among. I speak now of those whose lives are softened by the positions of their parents and who, educated and cultivated, perhaps talented or perhaps only impetuous, have been infected by the virus of revolt and have chosen to follow the precept that everything can be solved in street battles, using the most murderous weapons in the name of revolutionary ideas which coming events will either prove right or will alter.

The little Paris gamin in the majestic Square Court of the Louvre is as much at home there as if he owned the palace!

These children of the flower sellers who, on the first of May, while their parents hawk the traditional stalks of lilies-of-the-valley to bring good luck, play a game that would seem macabre if their little faces did not reflect the joy that their unaccustomed freedom from convention has brought them.

In the Luxembourg Gardens, older children leave their studies after another day in class, and mingle with workmen and small shopkeepers, looking for green grass and trees at the end of a day of mild weather, to read a little, to stroll, while the "small fry" of Saint-Germain-des-Prés play on the paths the same games as played everywhere: kickball, trundling a hoop.

The little boy on an empty street in the Fifth Arrondissement is firmly belted and buckled and helmeted, and he means to bring order into everything *at once,* in every suspicious corner of the capital where his services may be needed!

In the heart of a calm old man like me, all this evocation of the children of the city, which the tap roots of my life can never let go of, is part of what I call with tenderness My Paris, *Mon Paris.*

There are two kinds of time: time that is long and time that is short. Time in classrooms is an example of time that is long. It is so long that instructors have found themselves compelled to cut up an hour into sixty parts, further divisible into sixty smaller segments. This also gives the instructors the time to devise nasty, intricate problems that have no practical application whatsoever to a man's daily life.

— Doisneau

Pages 69, 70, and 71
The heights of Ménilmontant, at the
intersection of the Rue Piat and the Rue des
Envierges.
Pages 74 and 75
In the courtyard of the Louvre.
Pages 76 and 77
The flower sellers of the Madeleine.
Page 80
Sunday at the Tuileries.

4. THE GIRLS AND LOVERS OF PARIS

Once Paris held the monopoly on unabashed and even indiscreet lovers. Couples, plainly and simply in a fever about each other, married or not, kissed in public whenever they felt like it.

This did not bother anyone. Parisians were so used to the charming show that they watched it with a full understanding that love and gentleness were created in order to be practiced, and wherever such hunger showed itself.

How many of the sweethearts of Paris have I watched with my approving eye! Caught in their caresses, savoring them in the full light of day, they have not given a thought about the respectable people who might be offended by their young passion. How many times have I, halting now and then on my daily walk, stopped like any casual *voyeur* and enjoyed the spectacle of two lovely fresh mouths taking all the time they needed to taste what is, basically, the appetizer in the banquet of final possession?

I would not want to miss a shiver of their pleasure and my own, and sometimes, when the two lovers have emerged from their transport and have recognized me, by chance, I have not been able to stop myself from encouraging them with a heartfelt "Enjoy it while you can, my friends! Youth ends very quickly!" At this the two sweethearts usually hurl themselves back into another warm embrace, while I leave the rest of their spectators to applaud silently and continue my Paris stroll.

I used to be sure that I would always meet other lovers just as overt in other cities. But it was Paris herself, playing the tune for the rest of the world, the tune which Jean Cocteau said so correctly was "To know just how far to go." And one could not imagine that in London or New York any such show would be played out in public, nor anywhere but in this city of pleasure, Paris, the most gracefully depraved town in all the world.

But since those other days... since then things have changed, and my town has become almost chaste in comparison with London or New York!

Where did this new prudery come from?

First of all we can blame the United States, as usual, for it plainly stems from that enormous land of mixed races, that new world of physical and moral strengths unknown anywhere else that does not cease to inspire the youth of other countries.

In every sphere of activity (spatial, scientific, technical, sportive, artistic), this astounding nation built on pioneer stock, with its famous citizens superior in their bodily strength and natural energies, has set the pace for the rest of us earth people. Let us admit it honestly, no matter how justly or unjustly we have often felt free to criticize, as is commonly a need in the envious: It is a nation of champions.

And it is precisely this American vigor that suddenly upset the established balance of the French pattern of bodily enjoyment, so that the newcomers in the game began, themselves, to go much further than anyone could possibly have guessed in the evolution of modern sexuality.

Where have we all wandered since the time when my song "Valentine," which I sang at the Casino de Paris in 1925, made young ladies blush with its chorus? It said:

She had tiny little tootsies
Did Valentine,
My Valentine...
And she had tiny little titties
Which I tickled with my mitties—
Tra-la-la-la!
She had a tiny little chin
Did Valentine,
Ah, Valentine!
And besides her little feet, her
little tits, her
little chin,
She was as curly as a lamb....

The word that made all the trouble in this charming song by Willimetx and Christiné was *tétons*, a common French pet name for those two globes of love which, along with the face, make up the advance troops in feminine warfare. All of Paris, and then all of France, amused itself mightily with this one word, which, completely alive and vivid, almost seemed to conjure up the image of a naked, breathless young bosom.

When I first went there in 1928 to produce my own pictures, America was not at all shocked by "Valentine," simply because the song was impossible to sing in anything but French and one had to understand that language very well indeed to catch the impact of the famous little *tétons*. But back home, French radio demanded that on its air waves the word be replaced for a more innocent one, which, in Parisian slang, meant something like "nose" (*piton*). French mothers, horrified as they were supposed to be by the perversion inherent in the word "tit," altogether too descriptive, were being protected at the very breast of their innocent families!

Later, in 1930, when I was on tour in England, a large city censored the whole song—simply cut it out of my repertory "for reasons of obscenity." I was branded. How innocent these pretty little boobies of Valentine's were beside the indecencies which today we find perfectly correct and matter-of-fact!

Good old America! You sometimes upset us a little—and you will understand how the Parisians often feel that you outdo them in their sacred specialty, *l'amour!*

But believe me, for the time being and probably forever, Paris continues to celebrate *l'amour* everywhere: the streets, the café terraces, the pathways of the Bois de Boulogne and of Vincennes and all the city parks—and almost exactly in the same ways tried out by its girls and their lovers long before our sexual revolution—or the revolution of the sexes—reached its present peak.

We Parisians continue to practice love-making with that sense of proportion it seems to demand, when any of us wants to enjoy the most beautiful, the deepest, the most astonishing and the most intoxicating pleasure our Creator ever invented, to solace and comfort us for all the trouble we must go through simply to postpone dying too soon.

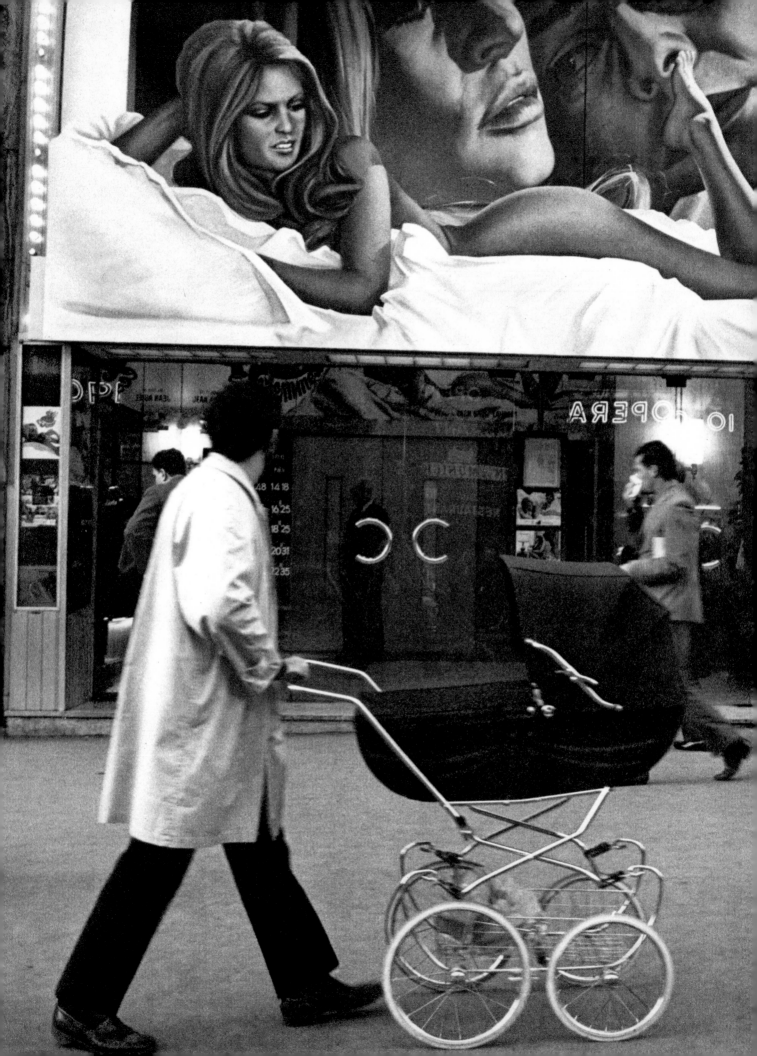

Page 86
The cloisters of the Palais Royal.
Page 87
Noon hour on the Rue de la Chaussée
d'Antin.
Pages 88 and 89
Place Vendôme.
Pages 92 and 93
The railroad bridge at the Ménilmontant
station.
Page 96
Maillol monument to Cézanne on the grounds
of the Tuileries.

5. THE STREETS OF PARIS

The streets and squares and avenues in my town make up the spectacle everyone advises a tourist to look at. They are the basis for the whole history of Paris, with its famous monuments, too rich, too numerous to count.

I know them all, for I have studied them with the pride of a true Parisian. But when thinking about the Paris of my own life, of my heart really, I must go directly into the narrow side streets of the city where special memories still linger for me. They may be of some of the moments of love which have left only sweet thoughts; they may be of professional moments of real pleasure and attainment; they may be of fleeting moments of simple tender humanity, good friendship, the sweet joy of true sympathetic company.

I have always been a stroller, an ambler, in the streets of my town, sniffing out its rich secrets. In French we call it "window-shopping" for want of a better translation, but it also means to become a part of the sidewalk crowds, so that you can observe touching or seductive strangers. It means involving yourself in speculation about what that man may do for a living, or what kind of existence this girl submits to. It involves quick pity for the feeble old couple clinging to each other as they totter along, trembling in their helpless wait for what life will do next to them. And then you must admire a pretty girl who passes by, her head high, and try to place her correctly in your private scale of merit: first class, second, plain dull. Willy-nilly you sum up the nonsensities of certain attitudes in the passers-by, are attracted to this one or that, feel a fleeting but keen excitement.

It is all this and more that you can experience, watching the spectacle of life shift and evolve in the streets. It is like a continuous movie that you understand and absorb according to your own sensitivities and to your skill at weighing other people by what your own life has taught you.

Suddenly you see a polio victim, dragged along in his chair, his gaze questioning—or dead. There is a blind man being led, or perhaps alone with his white cane. There is a lame man, a man on crutches. And all of them are handicapped, forced to find within themselves the strength to accept their lots.

I have always mooned along city streets like this, not only in Paris but on the main avenues of New York, Chicago, San Francisco, Los Angeles, Hollywood. I have loved all of it. It is as if seeing these samples of humanity pass before you will, *must,* make you understand that you have no right to feel sorry for yourself and your own life, ever—as if you must understand that the worst of any possible fate you see passing on the sidewalk might easily be your own, with a new turn of luck. Poof—it could happen like that!

It is essential that a man appreciates everything that gives him part of its beauty—of its grace, generosity, humility, simplicity. He must let it sink into him, breathe it. He must absorb everything that encourages him to stay alive and everything that seems to belong to his own idea of human dignity—and of plain courage as well.

The bodies and faces of the people of Paris have their own special characteristics. There is in any genuine "Parigot" a teasing sparkle in his eye, a kind of speed in his pace. And in his girl, true daughter of Eve, there is something completely feminine which may not be pure and total beauty but which breathes an indefinable perfume of desirability.

The rhythm of our existence has followed, in Paris, the same wild predestined course as elsewhere in the world. We are often, perhaps too often, involved deeply in this feverish race, but there is always, in even the most dramatic moments in our capital, a little teasing joke in the air, an unexpectedly bantering note, which might well make some innocent believe (but never trust it!) that at the bottom of the whole business nothing should be taken seriously.

In the Place de la Concorde, looking toward the Ritz Hotel, smile if you wish at the sight of seven pretty young girls led by a nun, who forget all their coquettish manners as they dash, elbows tight to their sides as is proper, but still more or less helplessly, in an awkward effort to escape the cars that bear down on them too fast. Speed! More speed!

Our Champs Elysées has gone along with all the evolutions of Broadway, Times Square, and London's Carnaby Street. But the worst sartorial eccentricities no longer surprise us, in Paris or anywhere. The only figures we give a second look at are invariably those of pretty young girls or women, whether in mini-mini skirts or tailored pantsuits with low belts, long hair blowing to their waists or perhaps cut like a boy-girl's, as they walk the once staid avenue. At the corner of the Boulevard Saint-Germain and the Rue Soufflot, in spite of all the noise and traffic it is the *girls* Parisians are watching, not the automobiles!

More and more as I take my long walks through the streets of My Paris I change my itineraries. I like the Champs Elysées, where tourists and our young people are in the majority. The new "drug stores," fairly well gallicized, are another teeming haunt of our young. The big movie houses no longer see the large crowds of the past, except on Saturdays and Sundays, but the sidewalk cafés still stay filled with people watching the ebb and flow of all the tides of helter-skelter humanity that make Paris a living thing and not a shrine.

It is easy to tell by faces and their expressions who are the tourists. It is even amusing to play at giving them each a nationality. I am sure that we Frenchmen must be just as easily identifiable when we travel in other countries. It is not simply a question of clothes, the cut of a pair of trousers or the length of a skirt: no, every country in the world follows pretty much the same fashions. It is, above all, the expression, the look, the way of moving one's face, by which every man carries his own national flag within him.

I have my own sentimental pilgrimages, which often draw me into the blind alleys and the little narrow winding streets and neighborhoods, and to the music halls both modest and imposing, where my heart picks up the tatters and snippets of wonderful moments long since past. Even at the Place de la Concorde, where without any help from a traffic policeman's white stick every nervous hurrying car stops, suddenly respectful, as a young and pretty mother, looking almost like a child herself, wheels her baby across the usually frantic street. It would be easy to think of such a baby as a kind of little Jesus, come back to us on earth to strengthen our faltering love for one another.

Before such loveliness, I feel my heart swell with pride, for the beauty that lies in the streets of My Paris.

"Hell" on the Boulevard de Clichy. Passing through this door is, for "le bon Bourgeois," a kind of provocation. One foot poised before the tempting descent into sin, he still maintains his respectability. This Doorway to Hell was created during "la belle époque," the time when Montmartre songwriters were boldly attacking the established order. Bold, but in a different way, was Guimard, who took his inspiration from plant forms, which he incorporated into the entrances of the then-new subway.

— Doisneau

A cynical French driver commented recently that it is becoming increasingly difficult to knock down a pedestrian in Paris because they have developed such remarkable reflexes. It now seems that foreign tourists are developing similar reflexes. It is a major test of their agility and courage to walk across the Place de la Concorde. At first it is empty. The strollers, full of confidence, step out onto the walkways, then suddenly, at 60 kms an hour, they are faced with a great flotilla of cars bearing down upon them, liberated by the green light. Since most of the sprinters are young, they demonstrate remarkable techniques. A few even seem amused by this game.

— Doisneau

6. PARIS BY NIGHT

I cannot write about nighttime Paris without finding myself far back in time, around 1906, for instance, when a group of us young singers and actors made their headquarters a café-restaurant in the Faubourg Saint-Martin that was run by a grand old girl named Madame Pagès. She seemed to feel that she was the mother of all of us fledgling professionals, girls as well as men, who met at her place every night after our shows. She bossed us, she stormed at us, she pushed us around like a dictator—and always with love.

On the nights when we felt that a good prowl was in the air (and in those days that meant heading for Montmartre), we left Madame Pagès' place in groups of five or six, all of us young blades of about the same age, and usually on foot to save money, to see how successfully we could pick up a few girls for nothing.

Montmartre at that time was the place in Paris where most of the night life went on, in countless bars and dives and pleasure houses. There were all kinds of people, trying to forget their problems with dope, alcohol, excesses. There were homosexuals: active, passive, kept men or plain prostitutes. There were as many Lesbians and of as many persuasions. We, the groups of young music-hall hams, acted more or less like parasites in these crowds concentrating on their own vices and intoxications.

Among the whores of every sex, all looking for a kindred brother or sister or simply carrying out their jobs as streetwalkers, we would wait for a signal from one of the girls who might be fed up with prowling hopelessly until dawn for a good client. Then, with luck, we would gain her generosity—and take what she would give freely to a passing sweetheart, a real heart throb and not a customer. That way, we got out of having to pay her the usual sum her pimp would charge.

This was far from admirable, I grant you! But we were a bunch of immature clowns, and not one of us could yet do much boasting about his pathetic conquests.

As penniless young singers and actors on the loose, we found real and dangerous competition in night clubs like El Gârron and Le Capitole, where the boys from Argentina hung out—and I mean the genuine Argentinians of those faraway times. They were elegant, handsome, very tough, irresistible Don Juans to the girls, and above all rich.

Often the little prostitutes on the sidewalks where they walked their beat along the Rue Notre-Dame-de-Lorette, egged on a good brawl between us hams and the South Americans, and nine times out of ten a young Frenchman would find himself lying there on the pavement, while the Latin victor offered his arm gallantly to the girl whose favors we had been vying for together.

Of course I am talking here about our personal hassles and involvements. There were also in Montmartre many other types of less overt entertainment, from L'Abbaye de Thélème, tops in the most perverted of night shows, through Le Rat Mort, a mixed bag, to Le Pigalle, where a program filled with beautiful undressed girls always excited the audience, filled with tourists there to forget their troubles in forbidden dangers. And there was the Moulin Rouge, of course, where the can-can flourished with all its shocking promises—shocking in 1906, that is!

On the Place Blanche there was a famous homosexual bar, Chez Palmyre, ruled over by a woman and managed by a handsome, sensitive man, Jean d'Albret, who was respected by everyone. Good singers performed there. The waiters, their trays aloft, sped among the tables like well-trained choir boys, harmonizing on the choruses of popular tunes.

And at the very top of the steep Butte Montmartre, looking down over all of la Ville Lumière, were the special joints where song and alcohol joined happily with the most adulterous love-making.

A long time later the Tabarin sprang up. It presented excellent nude shows, forerunners of our present Lido, and was successful from the start. It was a part of the gradual evolution in the night life of Paris.

Everything about this eternal hunger for entertainment after dark has been greatly modernized, speeded up, in our present time. It has been "show-manized," if there is such a word. And the same evolution, part of the Parisian and indeed life education of the show-biz kids we were in 1906, probably added its influence to the special kind of culture necessary to the soul of any true music-hall artist. Actually it is plain that My Paris has not changed much in its knowledge of how to intoxicate a man's spirit! The only difference, in my own case, is that now I find myself white-haired and therefore obliged, without regret (or do I really mean that?), to stop talking about the kind of life that went on for me so long ago, so long ago.

If I want to remain honest, I cannot hide the fact that by now "my" town at night is not what it used to be for me! The enjoyment of Paris after dark, the kind of fun that was part of my youth, has been radically transformed for me. A man in his eighties no longer rollicks through the clubs and *bistros* and discreet hideaways which are still routine with all younger lovers of nocturnal excitement.

Now I never go out at night except for something very special. Like the time Duke Ellington came to Paris for his seventieth birthday and asked that I, Maurice, be the one to present to him the greetings of our capital. Why did he choose me? Ah, it was simply because the Duke and I are old friends!

We first met in 1930. A famous Broadway producer, Charles B. Dillingham, asked me to sing, between two movies I was to make in Hollywood, for a few weeks in one of his New York theaters. Mr. Dillingham suggested that I select for my musical accompaniment the best of all the jazz orchestras then in style. A friend told me about Duke Ellington and his wonderful music at the Cotton Club in Harlem. I went to hear him, and my decision was quick and sure: the Duke and nobody else.

It was agreed that he and his boys (and even today some of his musicians are the same ones who, very young, worked brilliantly for him in the Thirties and stayed with him as he progressed) would occupy the stage for the first part of the show. For the second half, Ellington and his band would go down into the orchestra pit to accompany me in my repertory of songs.

We were completely sold out for the entire run. It was a triumph that seemed like the Duke's final leap up from a taut springboard, projecting him into the almost legendary international heights from which he has never descended.

And so, one winter night in 1969 I deserted my warm house and went to the Alcazar, a popular music-hall-restaurant in Saint-Germain-des-Prés in the Latin Quarter. There, in the most fashionable place of its kind in Paris, I had the honor—and that word cannot possibly be too strong—to present to the Duke one of my professional straw hats, with the best birthday wishes of all of Paris, including my own.

I made a little speech to him in English, which I translated into French as I went along, for people who might not understand his native tongue. I told him that I especially loved to have him turn seventy, because it reminded me of my own youth.

There were roars of laughter when the Duke cocked his new boater jauntily on his head and replied like the true gentleman he is, "Fancy me wearing your straw hat, when no other artist in the world can even fill your shoes!"

I almost choked with emotion.

Another rare evening on the town came a few weeks later: opening night of a new show at the Lido, where it has become a custom for me to take some part in the performance. The Lido floor show is, without contradiction, the best in the world for its lavish elegance, its exquisite girls, its talent and true quality. It is absolutely dynamic and without a rival.

The very day of the opening the Duke of Windsor, who has honored me with his friendship since the time when he was Prince of Wales, asked me to escort the Duchess, since he was worried about the effect of the photographers' flash bulbs on his eyes, temporarily strained.

I arrived right on the hour and the minute at their home, with just enough time to click my whisky glass to the Duke's before I offered my arm to his Duchess, and we headed for the supper revue at the Lido. You can imagine the whole scene: our arrival, the mob of people waiting to watch the celebrities go in, the cameras and TV crews.

I tried to appear very dignified as we entred but made the Duchess laugh when I murmured to her that my knees were invisibly shaking at the idea of substituting for a king. Gently she replied, "Don't worry, Maurice! You behave like one." Imagine! She said that to me! I spent an unforgettable evening with the Duchess, who proved to be simple, human and delightfully witty. I got home very late after this taste of Paris night life, which had passed like a dream before I sank into a deep sleep.

For the real lovers of a gay life-after-dark, Paris is bursting with places where it can be found in its full glory. There is Maxim's, where a night can seem to pass in minutes. There is the Folies Bergères, always tops. Or Zizi Jeanmaire at the Casino de Paris, in a show produced by her talented husband, Roland Petit.

Their last revue, brilliantly modern, gave Jeanmaire the awesome responsibility of appearing on the same stage where the unique Mistinguett made theatrical history in—well, some time ago! Edith Piaf played there, the most astonishing street singer Paris has ever acclaimed, in spite of her many physical handicaps—or perhaps a little because of them. Nobody ever takes the exact place of any other person. Each star is made differently. Jeanmaire, a fine dancer now turned singer, has within her the gifts which can permit her to come after people like "la Mist" and then "the Piaf waif," so that she may finally become plain "Zizi" to her public.

If you still feel frisky, there are plenty of "French striptease" places, and that means stripping right to the buff, which can absorb you until your eyes give out, along toward morning. And I know you will excuse me for not coming along as your guide! If I spent my nights now as I used to, I would soon be only a memory.

My dear friends, I have written about My Paris as frankly as I know how and with all the devotion of a son of the City of Light. Look again at the photographs in this book, and be as proud as I am to say, "I love you!"

The Saturday night dancers in this nightclub on
the Rue de Lappe, near the Bastille, are mostly
French, but you may spot a few tourists who have
discovered the place or been brought by their
Parisian friends. A popular weekend sport.

— Doisneau

Page 131
In the old quarter of the Bastille.
Page 132
Gilbert, the dragon of Montparnasse.
Page 133
Place de la Concorde.
Pages 136 and 137
Apache dancer in a Paris cabaret.
Pages 138 through 149
The night life of Paris. The Balajo, the
Alcazar—Saint-Germain-des-Prés or the Rue
la Lappe.
Pages 150 and 151
At the Casino de Paris, Roland Petit, Zizi
Jeanmaire and Maurice Chevalier.
Page 152
Another Statue of Liberty flashing from the
Grenelle Bridge over the Seine.

Design and Production by Chanticleer Press, Inc., New York
Monochrome gravure printing and binding by Conzett & Huber,
Zurich, Switzerland

Four-color offset printing by Offset & Buchdruck AG, Zurich, Switzerland